A STUDENT'S GUIDE TO
ECONOMICS

ISI GUIDES TO THE MAJOR DISCIPLINES

GENERAL EDITOR   EDITOR
JEFFREY O. NELSON   WINFIELD J. C. MYERS

A STUDENT'S GUIDE TO PHILOSOPHY
BY RALPH M. MCINERNY

A STUDENT'S GUIDE TO LITERATURE
BY R. V. YOUNG

A STUDENT'S GUIDE TO LIBERAL LEARNING
BY JAMES V. SCHALL, S.J.

A STUDENT'S GUIDE TO THE STUDY OF HISTORY
BY JOHN LUKACS

A STUDENT'S GUIDE TO THE CORE CURRICULUM
BY MARK C. HENRIE

A STUDENT'S GUIDE TO U.S. HISTORY
BY WILFRED M. MCCLAY

A STUDENT'S GUIDE TO ECONOMICS
BY PAUL HEYNE

A STUDENT'S GUIDE TO POLITICAL PHILOSOPHY
BY HARVEY C. MANSFIELD

A Student's Guide to Economics

PAUL HEYNE

Edited by
JOSEPH A. WEGLARZ
WALSH COLLEGE

ISI BOOKS
WILMINGTON, DELAWARE

The Student Self-Reliance Project and the ISI Guides to the Major Disciplines are made possible by grants from the Philip M. McKenna Foundation, the Wilbur Foundation, F. M. Kirby Foundation, Castle Rock Foundation, J. Bayard Boyle, Jr., the Huston Foundation, the William H. Donner Foundation, Pierre F. and Enid Goodrich Foundation, and other contributors who wish to remain anonymous. The Intercollegiate Studies Institute gratefully acknowledges their support.

Cataloging-in-Publication Data

Heyne, Paul.
     A student's guide to economics / by Paul Heyne.
     1st ed.—Wilmington, Del. : ISI Books, 2000.

       p. cm.

       ISBN 1-882926-44-7
       1. Economics—Outlines, syllabi, etc.
     I. Title. II. Title: Guide to economics.

HB171.5 .H49 2000   00-101238
330/.076—dc21   CIP

Published in the United States by:

     ISI Books
     Post Office Box 4431
     Wilmington, DE 19807-0431

Cover and interior design by Sam Torode

Manufactured in Canada

CONTENTS

INTRODUCTORY NOTE

WHAT IS ECONOMICS and what can you expect to learn from studying it? Those questions are harder to answer than you might suppose.

Dictionaries offer little help. The standard dictionary definition says that economics studies the production, distribution, and consumption of wealth, which is clearly not the case. Economics does not tell farmers how to produce wheat or instruct railroad managers on how to distribute it or advise consumers on the contribution whole wheat bread makes to an adequate diet. Economics studies only very limited aspects of the production, distribution, and consumption of wealth.

Paul Heyne

IN THE BEGINNING: ECONOMIC GROWTH AND RELATIVE PRICES

IF ECONOMICS BEGAN, as most (but not all) economists believe, with the publication in 1776 of Adam Smith's *Inquiry into the Nature and Causes of the Wealth of Nations,* then economics originated as an attempt to answer the question, What causes economic growth? The volume of a nation's annual production, Smith asserted, will depend primarily on "the skill, dexterity, and judgment" with which people apply their labor to the natural resources available to them, and this in turn will depend primarily upon the extent to which they have carried the division of labor, or what we would call specialization. But specialization requires trade, so that when the division of labor has extended itself sufficiently throughout a society, everyone lives by exchanging. Everyone, Smith wrote, "becomes in some measure a merchant," and the society becomes "a commercial society." Smith set himself the task of explaining how productive activity is coordinated in a commercial society.

The way in which Smith went about constructing his explanation established a major part of the agenda for his successors up to the present day. He saw that the wealth-producing activities of a commercial society are coordinated through movements in the relative prices of goods, both outputs and inputs. And so he had to explain how these prices are determined. For two centuries, the theory of relative prices has continued to be the core of economics. What is economics and what will you learn from studying it? You will learn first of all a theory of relative prices: how they come to be what they are and what effects they have. If Adam Smith is in fact the founder of economic science, it is primarily because he first set out this basic agenda.

His questions were better than his answers, however. Smith's theory of relative prices was fundamentally incomplete and inconsistent. He tried to explain the prices of goods by reference to their costs of production. But costs of production are themselves prices: the prices of labor, of natural resources and raw materials, and of previously produced goods that are used in the production process. The wages of a carpenter and the cost of lumber do indeed determine, at least in part, the price of a bookcase. But the prices people are willing to pay for bookcases and other goods that carpenters make out of wood also help determine the wage rates carpenters must be paid and the cost of purchasing lumber. Relative prices cannot be explained as a result of one-way causation, because everything depends on everything else. Smith had an inkling of this truth, as he showed

---

Smith, Adam (1723-1790), was born in Kirkcaldy, Scotland. His mother was the daughter of a prominent landowner and his father, who died before Smith was born, was the comptroller of customs. Escaping a reputed attempt by gypsies to carry him away when he was four, Smith entered the University of Glasgow at age fourteen and later studied at Oxford. In 1751, Smith was appointed professor of logic at Glasgow, and a year later moved into the chair of moral philosophy. Opportunities afforded him by the success of his *Theory of Moral Sentiments* (1759) allowed him to retire early and concentrate on his second book, *An Inquiry into the Nature and Causes of the Wealth of Nations.* Published in 1776, this work marks the beginning of serious analysis of economic phenomena (although the early beginnings of economic thought can be traced all the way back to the ancient Greeks, especially Xenophon's *Oeconomicus,* Plato's *Republic,* and Aristotle's *Politics*). It was Smith, more than any other writer of his age, who exemplified the high ideals of the Scottish enlightenment, with its focus on growth and development. Not only was his book a long-overdue diatribe against the principles and policies of a bankrupt economic system called mercantilism, Smith put into the hands of the general public a work of enduring importance which must be read by every serious student of economic thought. As the undisputed founder of the classical school of economics, Smith developed a theory of value, wages, rent, and profit, as well as a spirited defense of natural liberty and the free enterprise system. Smith did not deny the necessity of government but he assigned it only three legitimate roles: defense from attack by other nations, the maintenance of justice and order, and the erection and maintenance of public works and institutions. He is probably best remembered for his concept of the "invisible hand," according to which each individual is led to promote the general welfare whenever he seeks to promote his own welfare through commercial activity.

in some of his attempts to explain the evolution of particular prices over time. But he was unable to incorporate the concept of mutual determination into his general theory of prices. For about the next one hundred years, neither were his successors.

THE REFORMULATION OF ECONOMIC THEORY
❧

IN THE LAST QUARTER of the nineteenth century, economics was taken over by university professors. Academics do not readily tolerate incoherence or inconsistency, and by the end of the century they had shaped the theory of prices into the basic form that it has had ever since, the form that every economist, budding or mature, encounters when he undertakes the study of economic theory. They did so by employing simultaneously three insights that their predecessors had often grasped separately but had never been able to put together in an effective way. The first we have already mentioned: the recognition that everything depends on everything else, or what we may call the *mutual determination* insight.

The second was the *subjective* insight: there are no objective costs. Costs as well as prices (costs *are* prices) reflect subjective valuations. "Things" cannot have a cost. Only actions can have costs, and those costs will be costs *to the actor.* What is the cost of a college education, for example? The question cannot be answered. There is a cost of *providing* a college education, but also a quite different cost of *acquiring* a college education. The cost of acquiring a college education can mean the cost to the student who acquires it, or the cost to parents who pay for it, or even in some cases the cost to another student who was not admitted to the university because the student in question took the last slot available. From the economist's perspective, the relevant cost of taking any action is always the value to the actor of the opportunity thereby given up. Opportunity costs, as they are called, are the only kind of costs that affect decisions or prices.

The third insight essential to the formulation of a coherent theory of relative prices was the *marginal* insight. Which is more valuable: water or diamonds? Almost everyone who is asked that question will immediately answer, "Water." But when asked which they would take if offered their choice between a tumbler of water or a tumbler of diamonds, they hesitate. Then they defensively say something like, "I would take the water if I were dying of thirst in the middle of a desert." They are not, however, dying of thirst in the middle of a desert, and they would in reality choose the diamonds, because in almost every situation in which they might find themselves, the diamonds would be much more valuable to them than the water. The value of anything and everything depends upon the situation. Economists use the word *margin* to refer to the "edge" where decisions are made. The only value relevant to a decision is the marginal value, the *addition* to value (or subtraction from value) that is expected to result from making a specific decision in a specific situation, or *on a specific margin.*

THE INTRODUCTORY SURVEY

FOR A CLEAR AND INSIGHTFUL summary of what contemporary economics has to say about the world, consult *The Economist's View of the World: Government, Markets, and Public Policy,* written by political scientist Steven E. Rhoads. In the first two-thirds of the book, Rhoads introduces and explains the most useful concepts in the economist's theoretical tool kit and illustrates their application. In the remaining pages, he discusses the major limitations of the economist's perspective. This book is a splendid introduction to contemporary economics, as suggested by the many reprintings that have occurred since its first publication in 1985.

Where should you go next? If you intend to specialize in economics, you cannot avoid the courses your college or university offers. And that means you cannot avoid the textbooks your instructors choose. You must hope that they choose well. The standard introduction is a two-course sequence of microeconomics and macroeconomics, with the order of the two courses varying. Prior to the 1940s, these terms were unknown. The term *macroeconomics* was invented in the early 1940s to describe the analysis of the causes and cures of recessions, a concern that had come to dominate the discipline of economics as a consequence of the Great Depression. *Makros* is the Greek word for "large," and macroeconomics was the study of the forces supposedly controlling the behavior of the economy in the aggregate. Traditional economic theory, which explained the determination of relative prices and how changing prices assigned resources to their various tasks, was then dubbed microeconomics, from the Greek *mikros,* meaning "small."

THE NEGLECT OF RECESSIONS AND THE RISE OF MACROECONOMICS
❧

ADAM SMITH WAS NOT greatly concerned about the problem of recessions. He seems to have believed that alternating periods of booming sales with vigorous productive activity, and slumping sales with production facilities closed down and many workers unemployed, were either not a serious problem or else not a problem on whose causes and possible cures his analysis could shed any useful light. John Stuart Mill, writing seventy-two years after Smith, devotes a single chapter of his influential *Principles of Political Economy*—chapter 14 in book 3—to the problem of "general gluts" or "excess of supply." It would be wrong to say that Mill denied the possibility of recessions. But he certainly minimized their importance. He maintained that it was not possible for an economic system to produce too much of everything, and that when appearances seemed to indicate otherwise, we were simply viewing the results of mistakes that had been made by producers, which they would have to correct.

Mill's almost cavalier dismissal of the problems caused by mistakes and the necessity of subsequently correcting those mistakes exemplifies a striking fault that runs through most economic theorizing for almost two centuries after Adam Smith: the neglect of uncertainty. Economists have often reasoned about the operation of markets as if all the actors possessed all the knowledge they required to make decisions that they would not later come to regret. The interactions of demanders and suppliers were assumed to produce smooth and rapid movements of prices and resources to their equilibrium states, where all intentions are reconciled. While market processes do indeed coordinate the intentions of actors in a manner that could almost be called miraculous, it is not in fact a miracle, and it is consequently not as smooth and rapid as economists have too often assumed.

Demanders and suppliers make their decisions on the basis of expectations, and those expectations are regularly mistaken to a lesser or greater extent. If economic science is to explain market processes, it must take them as they are and not as they would be in some idealized world of perfect and costless information. Toward the end of the nineteenth century, professional economists began to give increasing attention to the problems of fluctuations in the purchasing power of money (the price level) and recurring periods of boom and slump in national economies. The two problems, they saw, were related. The behavior of banking and money systems at times generated more money and easier credit terms than were consistent with underlying conditions, which prompted business-decision makers to overexpand their investment and production activities, which created unsustainable levels of economic activity (booms), which eventually required correction in the form of production cutbacks and layoffs (slumps). How and why all this happened, how and why psychological factors and other forces external to the monetary system affected the process, and what kinds of institutional reforms might alleviate these patterns of alternating boom and slump—these issues were the subject of a great deal of research and reflection on the part of professional economists from the late-nineteenth century to the onset of the Great Depression in the 1930s. An excellent distillation of economists' thinking on these issues was published in 1937 by Gottfried von Haberler, in a work commissioned by the League of Nations and titled *Prosperity and Depression.*

Research and reflection on "the business cycle" or "the trade cycle" came to an abrupt halt toward the end of the 1930s, partly because of the outbreak of World War II, but primarily because economists were rushing to join the research agenda initiated by the 1936 publication of *The*

General Theory of Employment, Interest, and Money, by John Maynard Keynes. There have been many attempts to explain the spectacular success of this confused and confusing book, including some that make the very obscurity of the book a major factor in attracting the interest and attention of economists. A dominant factor in any plausible explanation has to be the failure of all other research programs to come up with an analysis of recessions that suggested a workable remedy at a time when a remedy was urgently desired. *The General Theory* had a cure as well as a diagnosis: government spending to make up the deficiency in private spending that had caused and was prolonging the slump. This was the essential message eventually extracted from *The General Theory* and presented after World War II in the macroeconomics portion of the theory sequences.

MACROECONOMICS
AND MICROECONOMICS

IN THE OPINION of its enthusiasts, macroeconomics was now one half of all economics. Paul Samuelson, who in 1970 became the first American recipient of a Nobel Prize in economics, published in 1948 the first edition of a textbook that came over the course of the next twenty years, through adoptions, imitations, and translations, to dominate the teaching of economics. *Economics: An Introductory Analysis* presented macroeconomics, or what Samuelson called "the modern theory of income determination," prior to its presentation of microeconomics, thereby implying that the study of booms and slumps could be undertaken without benefit of the concepts and theories of traditional economic theory. It was not necessary to understand how

---

SAMUELSON, PAUL A. (b. 1915), received his B.A. from the University of Chicago and his Ph.D. from Harvard University. He began teaching at the Massachusetts Institute of Technology in 1940 and has served as an economic consultant to the U.S. government on many occasions. Samuelson popularized the revolutionary economics of Keynes to millions of college students with his 1948 textbook, *Economics.* Although the thirty-three-year-old professor of economics did not claim to have furthered any one cause, the textbook reflected the prevailing orthodoxy of the day: the need for an activist government and deep reservations about the effectiveness of free markets. It is difficult to exaggerate the impact of Samuelson's text. Its fifteen lively and engaging editions have sold more than four million copies and it has been translated into over forty languages. Today, however, the Nobel laureate's message that government should correct market failures and provide public goods has lost much of its original punch. Paul Heyne's *The Economic Way of Thinking,* now in its ninth edition, has provided a more realistic and balanced approach for those students, as Samuelson wrote in his preface to the first edition, "who will never take more than one or two semesters of economics but are interested in the subject as part of a general education."

markets worked in order to understand why national economies underwent booms and slumps and what could be done (by governments) to control them. The processes of demand and supply for individual goods and services, not excluding money and credit, and the ever-changing relative prices generated by these processes, were mostly irrelevant to the understanding and control of recession or inflation. Macroeconomic analysis was conducted, at least by the enthusiasts and in the textbooks, in terms of aggregated variables such as total expenditures on personal consumption, total business investment, and total government purchases of goods and services.

There were always dissenters from this macroeconomic orthodoxy, but they tended to be dismissed in the early years as mere extremists of the Right or Left. While the empirical and theoretical investigations of these critics were gradually, if slowly, attracting support among professional economists, it was the events of the 1970s rather than ideas that effectively disrupted the complacent macroeconomic consensus. When unprecedentedly high rates of peacetime inflation occurred simultaneously with recessions in the 1970s, it was clear that explanations in terms of too much or too little aggregate demand could not explain what was happening. Economists started to return, often slowly and reluctantly, to the tools and concepts of traditional economic theory in order to construct microeconomic foundations for their macroeconomic theories. Economic theory began coming together once more after a long period of artificial division. Macroeconomics currently bears the marks of a building under reconstruction, up on jacks, even, until adequate microeconomic foundations can be inserted beneath it. A sign of all this is a gradual shift in college textbooks and courses from the Samuelson pattern of placing macroeconomics before microeconomics to a sequence in which microeconomics is taught first.

FROM THE EXCHANGE PROCESS TO THE ECONOMIZING PROCESS

ONE IMPORTANT CONSEQUENCE of the reformulation of economic theory which occurred at the end of the nineteenth century was a partial redirection of economists' interest in economic growth and the process of exchange, which was central in Adam Smith's inquiry, to the issue of efficiency and the process of economizing. The reformulated theory of relative prices was simultaneously a theory of resource allocation; hence, a correct statement of the theory amounted to an implicit statement of the conditions under which scarce resources were put to their most efficient uses, the uses that maximized net value. Economists began to identify *scarcity* as the fundamental problem with which their discipline dealt, and to assume that the appropriate response to the problem of scarcity was a more efficient allocation of resources. Maximum efficiency is achieved when all resources are so allocated among alternative uses that no additional net value can be created by any reallocation. The task of spelling out the formal conditions for achieving maximum efficiency, or an "optimal" allocation of resources, began to occupy a greater share of economists' attention.

This was probably the principal factor bringing about a

SAY, JEAN-BAPTISTE (1776-1832), was France's first economics professor. Born in Lyon, Say spent time as a businessman in England before returning to France to edit a magazine espousing the ideas of the French Revolution. In 1799, he was appointed to the Tribunate, one house of the Consulate, but he was eventually dismissed by Napoleon, who did not like his extreme laissez-faire views. Say's *Treatise on Political Economy* (1803) went through five editions in his lifetime, with translations used in universities in the United States as well as Europe. Often wrongly credited with the phrase "supply creates its own demand," (credit must instead be given to James Mill in his 1808 work *Commerce Defended*), Say's real importance stemmed from his ability to popularize the ideas of Adam Smith on the European continent.

gradual change in the name of the discipline from *political economy* to *economics*. "Political economy" had always been a misnomer. To the Greeks, economy (*oikonomia*) was the art of managing a household, and an economist (*oikonomos*) was a person entrusted with that responsibility. As the modern nation-state began to emerge in sixteenth-century Europe and ambitious men started constructing policies to enhance the power of the rulers whose interests they wished to serve, the term that came into use to describe their science or art was "political economy"—literally, the science or art of managing the state, the *polis,* as if it were a household. Jean-Baptiste Say probably deserves the credit (or blame) for first applying the term "political economy" to the new science that began to be systematically cultivated at the beginning of the nineteenth century. In 1803 Say published the first edition of *A Treatise on Political Economy,* which he subtitled, *The Production, Distribution, and Consumption of Wealth.* In this work he credits Adam Smith with originating the science of political economy by distinguishing it from the science of politics, demonstrating the method by which it must proceed, and establishing many of its most important truths. (How appropriate that someone named Jean-Baptiste should have christened the new science!)

But the term political economy was altogether inappropriate. It is a major theme of Adam Smith's *Wealth of Nations,* and an unstated assumption in the work of his successors, that states do not need political economists. It is hard to understand why Say, who was at least as insistent as Smith on the dangerous and delusionary character of attempts by government officials to manage the creation of wealth, chose to apply the name political economy to the science that was attempting to show how the members of society produced wealth without anyone managing the overall system. Political economists, understood as manag-

---

MILL, JOHN STUART (1806-1873), was the eldest son of James Mill, a published economist in his own right. James Mill, a demanding father, tutored his precocious son at home and on walks together; the younger Mill began learning Greek at three years of age, Latin at eight, and differential calculus at twelve. By the time he was nineteen he was already publishing scholarly articles. His *Principles of Political Economy with Some of Their Applications to Social Philosophy* (1848) was used as the major textbook of the English-speaking world until the publication of Alfred Marshall's *Principles of Economics* in 1890. Mill incorporated the utilitarianism of Jeremy Bentham and the intellectual rigor of David Ricardo into his examination of the economy. From an essentially Ricardian framework, Mill shed light on the concept of comparative costs and restated Adam Smith's "law of demand and supply" for a new age. In addition, Mill had a tremendous impact on the public policy issues of his day. An advocate of inheritance taxation, women's suffrage, and compulsory education (not schooling) for children, Mill's ideas were seen by many as instruments of social change.

ers or would-be managers of a nation's wealth-producing activities, were not needed. In 1831, while a professor of political economy at Oxford University, Richard Whately delivered a series of lectures which were published in the same year as *Introductory Lectures on Political Economy.* In these lectures, Whately suggested that political economy ought to have been called *catallactics,* the science of exchanges, from the Greek word for "exchange." John Stuart Mill agreed, but conceded that it was too late to change an established name.

As the attention of economists moved in the twentieth century from the exchange process to the economizing process, however, the name *economics* gradually came to be an accurate description of a major part of the discipline. Economics became much more technical and mathematical as economists worked out, often in mind-numbing detail, the conditions that would yield the most efficient allocation of resources for society as a whole.

WHO IS IN CHARGE?

THE CHANGE IN FOCUS raised an interesting question: *Who* manages the resources of the society or the nation?

When economics shifted its attention from exchange to economizing, it opened a door for the *political* economist to sneak back in. The most insistent critic of this development has been 1986 Nobel laureate James Buchanan. In a large number of his writings, and especially in an essay titled "What Should Economists Do?" Buchanan argues that the economizing perspective has tempted economists to suppose implicitly that there is some *one* point of view from which the overall allocation of resources can be assessed for its efficiency, and thus to see their own task as that of giving advice to a benevolent despot. Buchanan wants economists to accept the humbler task of using their understanding of the exchange process to suggest rules of the game, or constitutions, that will enable the members of a free society to cooperate more effectively. Thus he urges renewed attention to the exchange process and less attention to the economizing process.

The economist who probably did the most over the long run to persuade many economists that exchange and not economizing ought again to be the focus of their concern was Friedrich von Hayek, one of two recipients of the 1974 Nobel Prize in economics. The central error of economists, Hayek maintained in a brilliant essay published in

1945, was the assumption that all relevant knowledge could be *given* to decision makers so that determining the most efficient or "optimal" allocation of resources was simply a matter for mathematical calculation. Hayek's essay, "The Use of Knowledge in Society," argues that the fundamental problem for a modern economic system is how to use the knowledge of all the members of society, knowledge that is widely scattered, that cannot possibly be assembled in a way

---

MENGER, KARL (1840-1921), studied law and political science, mostly in Prague, and took his Ph.D. from the Jagiellonian University in Kraków in 1867. Soon after graduation he began a career in journalism. It was while he was a journalist that Menger became interested in economics, seeing a discrepancy between economic theory and economic events. In his *Principles of Economics* (1871), Menger pointed out that the only values important to the decision-making process are marginal and sub-jective, thereby setting off the marginalist revolution and finally unlock-ing the "paradox of value" problem that hindered the classical econo-mists of the eighteenth and nineteenth centuries. Menger was one of three thinkers that independently discovered the revolutionary prin-ciple of marginal utility (the others were the Swiss economist Leon Walras and the British economist William Stanley Jevons), which forms the basis of modern-day microeconomics. Instead of viewing the world in terms of land, labor, and capital (as the classical economists were apt to do), Menger saw the world much differently than his classical predeces-sors. He identified a number of higher-order goods that were trans-formed into lower-order consumer goods. This stages-of-production model was later reworked by his fellow Austrian Eugen Boehm-Bawerk into a complete theory of capital and interest. Menger is considered the founder of the Austrian school of economics.

that would allow it to be "given" to any manager of the economy, but that is nonetheless vital to the coordination of an order that effectively utilizes available means to satisfy the diverse wants of the members of society. While this knowledge cannot be assembled, its significance for decision making can be "published" in the form of the relative prices generated by the processes of supply and demand operating within a society characterized by private property rights and freedom to exchange. The relative prices that supply and demand processes produce are indicators of relative scarcity that individual economizers use to make their own decisions to demand or supply, decisions that when acted upon create new indicators of relative scarcity that then direct subsequent decisions.

In 1980 Thomas Sowell published *Knowledge and Decisions,* a book that he described as an extended commentary on Hayek's essay. Hayek himself called *Knowledge and Decisions* "the best book on general economics in many a year" and credited Sowell with "translating abstract and theoretical argument into a highly concrete and realistic discussion of the central problems of contemporary economic policy." The book is a remarkably lucid and comprehensive exposition of what economists know about the functioning of social systems, and it will amply reward the thoughtful reader.

IGNORANCE AND SELF-INTEREST

SOWELL USED A quotation from Walter Lippmann as the epigraph of *Knowledge and Decisions:* "Man is no Aristotelian god contemplating all existence at one glance." Who could disagree? And yet many *do* disagree, regularly and persistently, by presenting analyses of social problems and proposing remedies for these problems that implicitly assume we are or ought to be Aristotelian gods. They grossly underestimate the amount of detailed knowledge that has to be used to provide food and housing for the inhabitants of a city; to assure enough but not too many physicians, plumbers, poets, and airline pilots; to make electricity and telephone service available to everyone; to maintain processes of discovery that will provide new and valuable answers to old problems of discomfort, disease, and disaster.

The dramatic failure of socialism that could no longer be denied at the end of the twentieth century was not, as many seem to believe, a consequence of the fact that people are selfish and put their own interests ahead of the interests of society. It was a consequence of the fact that *no one is omniscient.* We put our own interests ahead of the interests of most of those with whom we interact because we know what our own interests are, but do not even know the identities of most of the people with whom we cooperate every day. Most of us behave courteously toward others. But we do not, because we cannot, put their interests ahead of our own. In families and perhaps in small face-to-face communities, it is possible for individuals to sacrifice their interests to the interests of others. But in the large and unavoidably

---

MARSHALL, ALFRED (1842-1924), studied at St. John's College, Cambridge University, where he distinguished himself in mathematics. After graduation, Marshall lectured at Cambridge, Bristol, and Oxford; his influence is illustrated by the fact that by 1888 half of the economics chairs in the United Kingdom were held by his students. Marshall published his *Principles of Economics* in 1890, a work that replaced Mill's *Principles* as the standard textbook for the next forty years. More than any other thinker of his time, Marshall attempted to make economics a science by introducing a number of mathematical and mechanical terms into his discussion (a mathematical appendix is included in the back of his work). His most famous contribution is that price is always determined by demand and supply, somewhat like the blades of a scissors. Other original contributions included his discussions on partial equilibrium analysis, price-elasticity of demand, consumer and producer surplus, internal and external economies of scale, quasi-rents, and the representative firm. Because he combined classical economics with marginalist thought, Marshall is considered the father of the neoclassical school of economics.

anonymous societies in which we produce for others and obtain from others most of what we need to live, our moral responsibility to others cannot be much more than to refrain from doing to them what we would consider unfair if done to us.

It is a common mistake, one unfortunately made by many economists when they are not thinking carefully, to assert that a market-coordinated economy encourages or rewards or depends upon *selfish* behavior. Markets coordinate *self-interested* behavior, which certainly may be selfish behavior, but much more frequently is not. Even to speak of self-interested behavior risks misunderstanding. Perhaps we ought to say that markets coordinate the behavior of people who are *pursuing the projects that interest them.* Those projects are large and small: finding a career and commuting to work; raising a family and getting milk into the refrigerator; alleviating the plight of the homeless and sawing lumber into appropriate lengths; providing better education for our children and painting lines on a crosswalk.

The basic principles of economics will not be readily understood or appreciated by people who believe that economic theory explains the operation of an essentially immoral society, one governed by selfishness or dominated by the desire for "material welfare" rather than "human welfare." What can those who contrast *material* with *human* welfare possibly have in mind? Material doesn't enjoy welfare; and human welfare is critically dependent on material "stuff," ranging all the way from human bodies through bread and cheese to the sound waves that enable us to converse with one another or enjoy the music of Mozart. People who talk this way literally do not know what they are talking about.

EXIT AND VOICE: MARKETS AND COMMUNITY

THE FACT THAT the most common moral criticisms of market systems reflect ignorance and misunderstanding does not mean that the critics are completely wrong. A major problem for market systems was pointedly described by the economist Albert O. Hirschman in a short book titled *Exit, Voice, and Loyalty* (1970). Hirschman suggests that there are two ways to induce institutions to conform to our wishes. One is to leave them if they do not. The other is to stay and argue. He calls the former option "exit" and the latter "voice."

Exit is the procedure associated with markets. If the local grocery store will not stock the kind of mustard we prefer, we go somewhere else. Voice is characteristic of politics. We do not leave the United States because government policy does not suit our preferences; we stay and we argue—or merely grumble if we don't think our efforts are likely to do any good. Between the two, exit tends to be preferred, as long as the cost of exiting is not too high, because it involves less hassle. Increasing wealth, with its accompanying expansion of markets and wider range of choices, has tended over time to reduce the cost of exit in many areas of our life. Compared to our parents, most of us can more easily leave our jobs for better ones, leave our neighborhoods for better ones, leave our religious communities for better ones, leave our spouses for better ones, and so on.

When the cost of exercising the exit option goes down, we have less incentive to stay and argue, and consequently less incentive and occasion to develop loyalty to people or institutions. We have more reason to "avoid commitments." The result of all this is that in a well-functioning market society, loyalties will tend over time to become shallower and less effective. Genuine communities will be harder to find or to maintain when found. Market systems, in short, generate powerful centrifugal forces within society, forces that tend to isolate individuals from one another, to substitute freedom of choice for the binding power of custom and tradition.

KEYNES, JOHN MAYNARD (1883-1946), was born in Cambridge, England, to professional parents. His father was an economist at Cambridge University, and his mother, one of the first women to graduate from the school, served as the city's mayor. Keynes attended Eton College and Cambridge, where he became a member of the Bloomsbury Group and studied under Alfred Marshall. Keynes eventually accumulated a fortune speculating in foreign currency and commodities, and in 1942 he became a baron: Lord Keynes of Tilton. Working within the Marshallian tradition, Keynes found much in the classical model wanting. His *General Theory of Employment, Interest, and Money,* published in 1936, offered new insights as well as criticisms of the orthodox model that was unable to shake the global depression of the early 1930s. It was Keynes who developed a new theory of income determination through his consumption function, a liquidity preference theory of interest rate determination, and a new explanation of the inflexibility of money wages. Keynes also advanced the notion that the ultimate determinate of economic growth is aggregate demand. The ability and willingness on the part of Keynes to work with aggregate microeconomic variables represented a drastic break from the way earlier economists looked at the economy. In addition, his emphasis on short-run analysis and his insistence on output or income levels to determine changing economic conditions rather than prices squarely put him outside the neoclassical camp. In the years immediately following World War II, Keynes's ideas found wide acceptance not only in academe but also among government policymakers. The view that government can achieve full employment and price stability by fine-tuning the economy through fiscal policy became almost universally accepted by all. Keynesianism had come of age. In a sense, it had become the new orthodoxy.

A lower exit cost has obvious advantages. People leave the villages where they were raised and move to the cities not only to find better opportunities but also to escape communities where their freedom is restricted because everyone knows what everyone else is doing. The dark side of this process is that in moving we also abandon the sources of support that can only be provided effectively within a community where indeed "everyone knows everyone else's business." Adam Smith observed that, in a market-coordinated society, everyone "stands at all times in need of the co-operation and assistance of great multitudes, while his whole life is scarce sufficient to gain the friendship of a few persons." But we don't need many friends in a well-functioning commercial society. We do not have to appeal to the *benevolence* of great multitudes to obtain the cooperation and assistance we want. The market enables us to appeal to their *self-regard*. It is a paradox of life in a modern, market-ordered society that people can become simultaneously more interdependent and more independent. Increasing specialization makes us more interdependent; but the market frees us from dependence on any particular persons and thereby makes us more independent.

Most of those who complain about the "immorality" of the marketplace have misread the situation. Market interactions are not less moral or more selfish than nonmarket interactions. But they are generally *more impersonal.* And that cannot really be changed without giving up the benefits derived from specialization: the greater range of more attractive choices that constitute an increase in wealth. If we decide to be dependent only on those whom

---

HAYEK, FRIEDRICH VON (1899-1992), educated at the University of Vienna and New York University, spent the majority of his teaching years at the London School of Economics and the University of Chicago. Hayek provided one of a number of dissenting voices during the Keynesian revolution. His *The Road to Serfdom* burst upon the world in 1944, warning all who would listen of the dangers of government economic planning. Even earlier, in London, Hayek had waged a war of words with Keynes (which Hayek subsequently lost), warning in his *Prices and Production* (1931) that without a proper understanding of the structure of production it was impossible to form a correct notion of the economy. Hayek criticized Keynes's belief in the power of the state to manage the economy. In contrast to Keynes, Hayek was a defender of the old order. He believed in a noninterventionist economic policy, especially during the Great Depression. He advocated a neutral monetary policy and assumed that market flexibility would realign prices and wages back to equilibrium. In addition, he saw through the "paradox of thrift" illusion of Keynes and favored policies that stimulated savings and advanced the virtue of thrift. Hayek not only defended the classical liberal tenets of the nineteenth century, but, as he demonstrated in his 1988 work *The Fatal Conceit,* looked forward with hope to the dawning of a new age, an age beyond Keynes and his muddled ideas.

we know personally, we will impoverish ourselves. If we want to retain and even expand the opportunities that make us wealthy, we must consent to be dependent on multitudes of people whom we have never even seen.

WEALTH, JUSTICE, AND FREEDOM

THOSE WHO ARE TEMPTED to suppose that the loss of community is too high a price to pay for the advantages of a market-coordinated economy should reflect carefully on the full range of benefits that "capitalism" has brought with it. The best available guide to such reflection is a small book written by Peter Berger, a sociologist with a special interest in economic cultures. In *The Capitalist Revolution: Fifty Propositions about Prosperity, Equality, and Liberty,* published in 1986, Berger carefully assesses the varied consequences of capitalism. He describes and evaluates not just the "toys" that it has created but also such "essential" goods as dental care and improved nutrition, as well as the political freedom associated with private ownership of property and the separation of economic decisions from government control. Anyone who is concerned about the loss of community in a market society, but then reads Berger's careful the record, will want to find ways to nurture community without destroying markets.

The moral critics of market systems often object at this point that such systems make no provision for *social justice*. Market systems allegedly accept what emerges from individuals' pursuit of their own interests and ignore the inequalities and injustices that this produces. Considered abstractly, that may be true. But market systems don't exist in abstraction; they are always part of a larger social system. And it is certainly not the case that societies that rely extensively on market systems ignore inequalities and injustices. Individuals, private groups, and governments regularly use the wealth that market systems generate to provide many kinds of assistance to persons who have fared poorly in those systems. Ask yourself whether the repudiation of market systems in the twentieth century produced more social justice, however we choose to define that slippery notion, than one finds in societies with full-fledged market systems. The poor receive less income than the rich in a market system; but the rise of market systems has arguably conferred its largest benefits on the poor, making the poverty of those who are least well-off under a market system the envy of people in societies where markets have not flourished.

Friedrich von Hayek has written a penetrating critique of those who misuse justice arguments to attack market economies in *The Mirage of Social Justice,* a book published in 1976 as the second volume of his trilogy on *Law, Legislation, and Liberty.* Hayek has sometimes been misunderstood to be arguing that social justice is a meaningless concept—a misunderstanding for which he himself is largely responsible. But what he actually means is that no human being or group of human beings knows enough to decide what would constitute a just allocation of resources, and no one who claimed to possess such knowledge could, consistent with justice itself, be granted the power to enforce such an allocation. We must be content with establishing just rules, just procedures. If the results are unsatisfactory and we want to change them, either through private action or through government, we must do so in ways that are *not unjust,* which means in ways that do not violate just procedures. And what are "just procedures"? They are procedures consistent with the "rules of the game," the promises and commitments that we have made to one another, both explicitly and implicitly, through existing laws, the formal constitutions that underlie these laws, and the moral consensus which undergirds any workable constitution and defines a particular society.

Surveys of academics regularly indicate that economists are much more "conservative" on average than academics in the other social sciences. This results in large part from the fact that the public identifies support of market-coordinated economic systems with conservatism and that economists, who have specialized in the study of market systems, tend to have a much more favorable view of them than do other intellectuals. It is unfortunate that this kind of conservatism has also come to be associated in the public mind with an indifference to poverty. Far too many "people of goodwill" show very little goodwill toward those whose study of economics has persuaded them that a large society *cannot* be managed in the way that a household can be managed, and that poverty cannot be eliminated or even reduced merely by passing laws to prohibit the payment of low wages or the charging of high rents for residential property. In a large society, where people (*all* people) pursue the projects that interest them, *incentives matter greatly.* Even professional economists, who ought to know this, have often fallen so far under the intoxicating influence of the economizing perspective as to suppose that political economists can govern the world.

Milton Friedman, winner of the 1976 Nobel Prize, is widely known as a "conservative" economist. He has long seen himself, however, as a liberal, because he places a high value on the liberty of individuals, and as a radical, because he wants public policy initiatives to probe to the root (*radix,* in Latin) of the problems with which they are intended to deal. His 1962 book *Capitalism and Freedom* demonstrates both his liberal and his radical leanings. It also shows that economic theory can be effectively deployed to suggest public policies that will benefit almost everyone in the society, including many low-income victims of special interest legislation. Today, Friedman's book seems less radical than it appeared to be at the time of original publication. In 1962, Friedman's arguments for tuition vouchers, the privatization of Social Security, the elimination of regulations supposedly designed to protect consumers but actually employed to protect those in the regulated industries, and other systemic changes struck most readers as too radical to be politically realistic. It is a measure of how much we have learned in the intervening years, much of it from Friedman himself, that so many of these proposals have been adopted politically and the rest are at least under serious discussion.

Paul Heyne

ORGANIZATIONS AND MARKETS

ONE OF THE MISTAKES that people regularly make is to assume that government always pursues the public interest. An important branch of economics, usually known today as public choice economics, developed in the 1960s to question this assumption. In 1962, James Buchanan and his colleague Gordon Tullock laid important groundwork for subsequent research into the economics of politics when they published *The Calculus of Consent: Logical Foundations of*

BUCHANAN, JAMES (b. 1919), was born in Murfreesboro, Tennessee, the grandson of a populist governor. A World War II veteran, he received his Ph.D. at the University of Chicago and has taught at a number of universities, including the University of Virginia, Virginia Polytechnic Institute, and George Mason University. Buchanan is regarded as the founder of the Public Choice school of economics, a school that developed in order to analyze the phenomenon of the increasing role of government in the lives of individuals through the supply of more and more public goods. In his path-breaking work (with Gordon Tullock) entitled *The Calculus of Consent* (1962), Buchanan began to form the opinion that individuals are as rational in their interactions with government as they are in their own economic affairs. Government, therefore, is not an agency for good or bad; it is rather an agency by which individuals achieve their economic goals through politics. In fact, Buchanan maintains that governmental failures exist, sometimes on a grander scale than market failures, and must be included in any discussion or analysis of policy.

Constitutional Democracy. Soon after, in 1965, Mancur Olson published *The Logic of Collective Action,* a modestly sized book that continues to offer an accessible and reasonably complete survey of what economic theory has to say about the problems of group behavior and government actions. The fundamental insight of public choice economics is the fundamental assumption of all economic theory: Social phenomena, including political phenomena, emerge from the actions and interactions of individuals who are choosing in response to expected benefits and costs to themselves. It is a serious if common mistake to suppose that government, simply by virtue of its duty, cares for the public interest. The political challenge for the members of any society is to establish institutions that will so motivate and constrain public officials that they do in fact behave in ways that promote the public interest.

Here and elsewhere, economics in recent decades has been probing more deeply into the working of social institutions. An economist who provided a major impetus in this direction is Ronald Coase, the 1991 Nobel laureate, who raised the question as long ago as 1937 (in an article titled "The Nature of the Firm") of why the economic universe contained both firms and markets. Why do we organize and coordinate economic activity through decentralized markets instead of through centralized, hierarchical control? If the reason is that decentralized markets are necessary to reconcile information with incentive, why do firms exist? Why do businesses organize and coordinate their activities through hierarchical control instead of through decentralized markets? The answer Coase gave was that there are costs associated with the organization and coordination of economic activity, whether through markets or through firms. The undertakers of economic activities pay attention to these relative costs, which have come to be known as *transaction costs,* in deciding whether to employ markets or hierarchical control.

Economists paid relatively little attention to Coase's argument at the time. Twenty-three years later he published another article, titled "The Problem of Social Cost," in which he argued that the specific way in which property rights were assigned would have no effect on the allocation of resources *if transaction costs were zero.* Rights would simply change hands as the holders of the rights worked out contracts that placed all resources into those uses that maximized net value. But transaction costs are *not* zero.

And so decision makers are constantly searching for arrangements that will achieve their objectives while minimizing the costs of securing the cooperation of others: finding people with whom to transact, settling the terms of the transactions, monitoring the transaction agreements to assure compliance. By neglecting these costs, economists were indulging themselves in what Coase referred to as "blackboard economics": creating and then solving problems of inefficient resource use that only existed in the theoretical constructions of economists. *The Firm, the Market, and the Law,* published in 1988, reproduces Coase's seminal articles and presents, in the title essay of the book, his argument calling for an economics less interested in arid technique and more concerned with the institutions that evolve as people try to reduce transaction costs.

ECONOMIC GROWTH ONCE AGAIN

AFTER WORLD WAR II, when the European powers were freeing (discarding?) their colonies in Asia and Africa, professional economists began to think about ways in which these generally poor societies might rise to a tolerable level of wealth and well-being through the process of economic growth. Exuberant confidence was the order of the day, and "growth economists" constructed elaborate models to show how self-sustaining economic growth could be initiated in "underdeveloped countries." Not much more was supposedly required than a good economic model and a modest amount of financial aid from the developed countries, aid that these countries ought to provide because they could easily afford it and because it was in their interest to promote economic growth in poor countries and thereby prevent destabilizing and dangerous revolutions.

Peter Bauer and Basil Yamey published a book in 1957, *The Economics of Under-Developed Countries,* that calmly and systematically exposed the fallacious assumptions undergirding most "growth economics" of this period. Merely by reflecting carefully on the grander concepts of the growth economists, applying the basic tools of economic theory, and looking at some of the accumulated evidence, they drastically deflated the pretensions of those who thought that economic growth could be easily engineered. But they also deflated hopes, and that was a risky move. Those who believe that poverty can be cured by goodwill plus a bit of social engineering by political economists do not look kindly on those who demonstrate that it just isn't so. But Peter Bauer persisted—he clearly enjoyed a good scrap—and continued to publish books and articles aimed at demolishing the ideas of those who thought that Western economists and politicians could construct in underdeveloped countries a royal road to economic growth. *The Economics of Under-Developed Countries* and many of Bauer's subsequent publications provide an excellent introduction to applied economic theory as well as a fascinating record of controversy.

By the end of the twentieth century it was abundantly clear that Bauer had been basically correct. Economic growth depends upon the attitudes and knowledge of people and upon appropriate institutions, especially governments that secure private property rights and allow individuals to choose the ways in which they will employ the resources under their control. *Institutions, Institutional Change, and Economic Performance* (1990), by 1993 Nobel laureate and economic historian Douglass North, indicates in its title how far removed it is from the engineering models of the postwar years. *The Wealth and Poverty of Nations* (1998), by economic historian David Landes, is an engagingly written confirmation of much of what Bauer has argued for over the course of four decades.

Paul Heyne

THE STRANGE NATURE
OF ECONOMIC THEORY

ॐ

FRANK KNIGHT may be the most penetrating and critical thinker who ever devoted himself to economic theory, and the one indispensable book for those who wish to understand how a market-coordinated economy handles the problem of coordinating activity in the presence of uncertainty is Knight's *Risk, Uncertainty, and Profit,* first published in 1921. A surprising number of recent advances in the economic theory of institutions were anticipated in this remarkable book.

Knight often suggested in his later writings that economics had very little to say that was both true and relevant about the making of policy. But that little, he insisted, was vitally important, and he wanted economists to say it concisely and clearly and thereby clear the way for the discussion of important issues. This is an interesting position that every budding economist at least ought to consider.

Knight maintained that the basic propositions of economic theory were not so much derived from experience, much less from experiments, as they were fundamental truths that would become obvious to anyone who reflected

economics assumes rational behavior? But what is irrational behavior—other than behavior that seems to violate some cherished law of economics?

We shall not attempt to answer these questions. Our purpose in introducing them is simply to point out that economists use far more theory and use it with more confidence than they could ever justify on the basis of empirical studies. While many economists insist that economics is a science only insofar as it confirms its theory with empirical investigations, others maintain that empirical studies can only illustrate the theoretical truths of which economists are far more certain than they are of any relationships based on mere observation. Thus while some economists, usually those most keen to insist that economics is a True Science, look for proofs and disproofs, others say that it is the economist's task to use theory and empirical knowledge to tell "plausible stories." For example, why do commercial airlines give such huge discounts to passengers who stay over a Saturday night? A plausible response is that they are trying to distinguish between business travelers, whom they can charge a very high price, and leisure travelers, who won't fly at all unless they receive a much lower price.

Perhaps the most interesting—and for many economists

the most disconcerting—work on the methodology of economics to be produced in recent years has come from the pen of Deirdre (formerly Donald) McCloskey. McCloskey has argued in a series of brilliantly written articles and books that there is no such thing as *the* scientific method; that the task of scientists, including economists, is to persuade others of the truths that they believe they have discovered; and that economists ought therefore to abandon their search for the One True Argument and instead concern themselves with effective and responsible rhetoric. In *The Rhetoric of Economics,* published in 1985, McCloskey laid out these arguments and applied them to current controversies within economics.

Standard economic theory explains and predicts most effectively when actors know the costs of their supply decisions and can expect those decisions not to affect the demand for what they are offering. Consider the case of a seller who knows with great accuracy the cost to himself of offering for sale various alternative quantities of the good he supplies and how many units of his good consumers would be willing to purchase at different prices. Using this information he can calculate precisely the amount he wants to supply and the price he wants to charge.

But now suppose that he has competitors who monitor his behavior and adjust their own actions to take account of his decisions in ways that alter the demand for what he is selling. Then the correct decision for him to make will depend upon the decisions of others that are going to be based in part on his own decisions. The correct thing for him to decide to do may depend upon what others expect him to do and upon what he expects them to do in anticipation of what they expect him to do. Such situations are quite common in the world of business firms searching for the most profitable prices to set. They seem to introduce a

---

FRIEDMAN, MILTON (b. 1912), the fourth child of Austro-Hungarian immigrants, was raised in Rahway, New Jersey. With help from a competitive scholarship, Friedman worked his way through Rutgers University, initially intending to become an actuary. While at Rutgers he became interested in economics, eventually completing a controversial doctoral dissertation on doctors' high salaries. Friedman was the leading protagonist of the monetarist revolution (1956-1975), which later contributed to the demise of Keynesian economics. Friedman is best remembered for his criticism of the Phillips curve, which held an inverse relationship between the level of unemployment and the rate of inflation; his suggestion for a nondiscretionary rate of increase in the money supply at the economy's underlying rate of growth (i.e., Friedman's monetary rule); and his unabashedly strong defense of freedom and its positive effects on economic growth in *Capitalism and Freedom* (1962). Friedman is considered the leading spokesman for the Chicago school of economics.

fundamental indeterminacy into the relatively determinate world of supply, demand, and prices.

Economists have been experimenting for more than half a century with a different kind of theory that has the capability of injecting a measure of determinacy into such interactions. It is known as *game theory* because it deals with situations in which the appropriate strategy for any one player depends in part upon the strategy adopted by other players, who of course are choosing their own strategy with an eye on the strategy they expect others to adopt. Interest in game theory has increased substantially in economics in recent years, and any student pursuing graduate studies in the field can expect to encounter it. To what extent game theory will supplant or merely supplement theory of the standard kind is still very much an open question.

CONCLUDING COMMENTS

ANYONE WHO WANTS to become a professional economist today will have to be far better trained in mathematics than is the typical undergraduate in American colleges and universities. An undergraduate major in mathematics is more likely to get you into the graduate school of your choice than is an undergraduate major in economics. Those who run graduate education programs today seem to believe that an adequate knowledge of economic theory and economic institutions can be easily imparted to any bright graduate student with a command of mathematics, but that the reverse is not true. And a command of mathematics is essential for anyone who wants to master the theoretical and empirical articles that fill the professional journals.

How much of this literature helps anyone to understand the real world or to formulate better economic policies is at least debatable. In 1999 Daniel Klein edited *What Do Economists Contribute?,* a collection of nine essays by distinguished economists, prefaced by his own illuminating introductory essay. Anyone who is considering the possibility of specializing in economics ought to read this small but richly rewarding book, in which thoughtful economists reflect on what the profession does and what it ought to be doing. Something close to the following consensus emerges from the articles. Economists can make extremely valuable contributions to social welfare, but only with great difficulty. Few people understand how a commercial society succeeds in coordinating the innumerable projects that people pursue and in producing intricate cooperation from the pursuit of individual interests. As a consequence, popular fallacies abound, resist refutation, arise again later after they have been refuted, and create policy demands that politicians find difficult to resist. Many economists respond by writing and speaking only for other economists, in order to advance their professional careers; and those who do choose to address the general public too often choose the easy course of serving the spirit of the age or even well-organized special interests rather than risking the obloquy that might result from resisting popular or "progressive" initiatives. In addition, the articles suggest that economists can make valuable contributions to society by loving the truth more than popularity and by fashioning simple examples and stories to convey the vital insights of economic theory to the members of a democratic society.

That is not the view universally held among contemporary economists. It may even be a minority view in a discipline that has become increasingly preoccupied with itself. But in a free and democratic society, public policies cannot be simply imposed from above. They must ultimately be accepted by the people and by those the people choose to represent them. In a very important sense, the members of a democratic society obtain the public policies they deserve. It is the vocation of those who come to economics in the twenty-first century intending to do good—and not merely to do well—to improve public understanding of the commercial societies in which we live.

Paul Heyne

BIBLIOGRAPHY

Peter T. Bauer. *Dissent on Development: Studies and Debates in Development Economics.* London: Weidenfeld and Nicolson, 1971.

Peter T. Bauer. *Equality, the Third World, and Economic Delusion.* Cambridge, Mass.: Harvard University Press, 1981.

Peter T. Bauer and Basil S. Yamey. *The Economics of Under-Developed Countries.* Chicago: University of Chicago Press, 1957.

Peter L. Berger. *The Capitalist Revolution: Fifty Propositions about Prosperity, Equality, and Liberty.* New York: Basic Books, 1986.

James M. Buchanan. *The Limits of Liberty: Between Anarchy and Leviathan.* Chicago: University of Chicago Press, 1975.

James M. Buchanan. "What Should Economists Do?" *Southern Economic Journal* 30, no. 3 (January 1964): 213-222.

James M. Buchanan and Gordon Tullock. *The Calculus of Consent: Logical Foundations of Constitutional Democracy.* Ann Arbor: University of Michigan, 1962.

Ronald H. Coase. "The Firm, the Market, and the Law." In *The Firm, the Market, and the Law,* Chicago, University of Chicago Press, 1988.

Ronald H. Coase. "The Nature of the Firm," *Economica* n.s. 4 (November 1937): 386-405.

Ronald H. Coase. "The Problem of Social Cost." *Journal of Law and Economics* 3 (1960): 1-44.

Milton Friedman. *Capitalism and Freedom.* Chicago: University of Chicago Press, 1962.

Milton Friedman. "The Methodology of Positive Economics." In *Essays in Positive Economics,* Chicago, University of Chicago Press, 1953.

Milton Friedman and Rose Friedman. *Free to Choose: A Personal Statement.* New York: Harcourt, Brace, Jovanovich, 1980.

Milton Friedman and Anna Jacobson Schwartz. *A Monetary History of the United States, 1867–1960.* Princeton, NJ: Princeton University Press, 1963.

Gottfried von Haberler. *Prosperity and Depression: A Theoretical Analysis of Cyclical Movements.* Geneva: League of Nations, 1937.

A Student's Guide to Economics

Friedrich A. von Hayek. *The Constitution of Liberty*. Chicago: University of Chicago Press, 1960.

Friedrich A. von Hayek. "Economics and Knowledge," *Economica* n.s. 4 (February 1937): 33-54.

Friedrich A. von Hayek. *The Mirage of Social Justice*. Vol. 2 of *Law, Legislation, and Liberty*. Chicago: University of Chicago Press, 1976.

Friedrich A. von Hayek. "The Use of Knowledge in Society," *American Economic Review* 35, no. 4 (September 1945): 519-530.

Albert Hirschman. *Exit, Voice, and Loyalty*. Cambridge, Mass.: Harvard University Press, 1970.

John Maynard Keynes. *The General Theory of Employment, Interest, and Money*. London: Macmillan, 1936.

Daniel B. Klein, ed. *What Do Economists Contribute?* New York: New York University Press, 1999.

Frank H. Knight. *The Ethics of Competition and Other Essays*. New York: Harper & Bros., 1935.

Frank H. Knight. *Risk, Uncertainty, and Profit*. Boston: Houghton, 1921.

David S. Landes. *The Wealth and Poverty of Nations: Why Some Are So Rich and Some So Poor*. New York: W.W. Norton, 1998.

Steven E. Landsburg. *The Armchair Economist: Economics and Everyday Life*. New York: Free Press, 1993.

Alfred Marshall. *Principles of Economics*. London: Macmillan and Co., 1890.

D. N. McCloskey. *Knowledge and Persuasion in Economics*. Cambridge: Cambridge University Press, 1994.

D. N. McCloskey. *The Rhetoric of Economics*. Madison, Wis.: University of Wisconsin Press, 1985.

John Stuart Mill. *Principles of Political Economy, with Some of Their Applications to Social Philosophy*. London: J.W. Parker, 1848.

Ludwig von Mises. *Human Action: A Treatise on Econmics*. New Haven: Yale University Press, 1949.

Douglass C. North. *Institutions, Institutional Change, and Economic Performance*. Cambridge: Cambridge University Press, 1990.

Mancur Olson. *The Logic of Collective Action: Public Goods and the Theory of Groups*. Cambridge, Mass.: Harvard University Press, 1965.

Paul Heyne

Steven E. Rhoads. *The Economist's View of the World: Government, Markets, and Public Policy.* New York: Cambridge University Press, 1985.

Paul Samuelson. *Economics: An Introductory Analysis.* New York: McGraw-Hill Book Co., 1948.

Jean-Baptiste Say. *A Treatise on Political Economy, or the Production, Distribution and Consumption of Wealth.* Boston: Wells and Lilly, 1821.

Adam Smith. *An Inquiry into the Nature and Causes of the Wealth of Nations.* Dublin: Whitestone, 1776.

Thomas Sowell. *Knowledge and Decisions.* New York, Basic Books, 1980.

Richard Whately. *Introductory Lectures on Political Economy.* London: B. Fellowes, 1831.

Philip Wicksteed. *The Common Sense of Political Economy: Including a Study of the Human Basis of Economic Law.* London: Macmillan, 1910.

AFTERWORD

ቒ

PAUL HEYNE: AN APPRECIATION

BY THOMAS J. DILORENZO

Editor's Note: With the passing of Paul Heyne on March 9,
2000, the economics profession has lost an ardent champion of
the free enterprise system. Not only was Heyne regarded by his
students and friends as a fine teacher and lecturer at the
University of Washington, he was able to reach many more
students by way of his popular textbook, The Economic Way
of Thinking. *Its readability and integrative approach (i.e.,*
examining micro- and macroeconomic issues and problems
simultaneously) has made it the introductory choice among
many colleges and universities.

Paul Heyne

Paul Heyne graduated from Concordia Lutheran Seminary in St. Louis, received his M.A. in economics from Washington University in St. Louis, and took his Ph.D. in ethics and society from the University of Chicago. He began his teaching career in 1957 at Valparaiso University in Indiana. In 1966, he joined the faculty of Southern Methodist University, and in 1976 took a post at the University of Washington, where he remained until his death. It was at the University of Washington that Heyne began work on The Economic Way of Thinking.

Heyne was not only interested in economic questions; he also explored the ethical nature of business. As a devout Christian and theologian, Heyne took the role of the businessman with particular seriousness. According to Heyne, it was a challenge to be involved in the everyday activities of business without forgetting its ethical side. Much of this discussion can be found in his Private Keepers of the Public Interest, *published in 1968. As Heyne stated in the final chapter of his work, "business is not busy-ness, and zest does not imply mindless activism.... The businessman will reflect upon his achievements, but always remembering that the greatest achievement of a man is to become the full measure of his own potentiality."*

The following afterword (reprinted here by permission from

Ideas on Liberty*), by Thomas J. DiLorenzo, adjunct scholar of the Mises Institute at Auburn University and a professor of economics at Loyola College in Maryland, summarizes some of Heyne's primary contributions and in so doing provides an elegant eulogy for the man and his work.*

M OST AMERICANS have probably never heard of University of Washington economist Paul Heyne, who recently passed away. That's a shame, for Paul was arguably the most effective economic educator in America for the past twenty-five years.

Most free-market economists consider Heyne's textbook, *The Economic Way of Thinking,* to be by far the most effective tool for teaching the principles of economics. During the 1960s and '70s that honor resided with *University Economics* by UCLA economists Armen Alchian and William Allen, whom Professor Heyne acknowledged as his inspiration. The approach of Professors Heyne, Alchian, and Allen differs significantly from the dominant mainstream approach, which is almost exclusively devoted to a mind-numbing rendition of technique after technique in which students are forced to more or less memorize hundreds of theorems, formulas, and diagrams. Students inevitably become lost in the fog of technique, and most of them are miseducated.

In contrast, Paul Heyne believed that principles of economics must be taught "as tools of analysis." This means first picking an *application* of economic theory (the minimum wage, trade disputes, merger waves, price controls, exchange rate fluctuations, traffic congestion, and so on), and then explaining the unique contribution that economic theory makes to understanding the application. Once a particular economic theory is introduced in this way, *The Economic Way of Thinking* applies the same theory to several other applications. Heyne believed this is the only way that students can truly learn not just economics but *the economic way of thinking*.

His book went through nine editions over the past twenty years, but was never quite a market leader. One likely reason for this is stated by Heyne in his preface: teaching people to think like economists requires one to become familiar with both current economic events as well as economic theory, and to be able to apply that theory to myriad contemporary issues. Most academic economists are, well, too lazy for that. They prefer instead to take the easy way out and just recite a theory or two a day, accompanied by elaborate diagrams and mathematical manipulations that they long ago memorized.

POPULAR IN THE OLD SOVIET BLOC

The Economic Way of Thinking became enormously popular in the former communist countries in recent years, and Heyne himself spent a considerable amount of his time as an invited lecturer before audiences of Russians, Czechs, Slovaks, Hungarians, Bulgarians, Poles, and Romanians, among others. These are people who "can't afford to spend time learning an economics that is merely intellectual aerobics," he explained in the preface to his eighth edition; they "need to understand how markets work and what institutions are essential if effective cooperation is to occur in a society characterized by an extensive division of labor."

That is exactly what *The Economic Way of Thinking* teaches and what most other textbooks fail quite miserably at. That is because Heyne's vision of what economics is all about has its roots in Adam Smith; the Austrian school economists, most notably Nobel laureate F. A. Hayek; and Nobel laureate James M. Buchanan (a fellow traveler of the Austrian school). To these men, what matters and what most ordinary people do not understand is the process of exchange:

the process by which literally millions of people in society coordinate their plans through markets—as long as they possess the freedom to do so. How this process works "is the great puzzle that the economic way of thinking begins to resolve," and few people have ever done it better than Paul Heyne.

FOCUS ON EXCHANGE

Focusing on market exchange through social cooperation and the division of labor—as opposed to mere "economizing" behavior, which is the subject of most economics texts—forces one to learn the importance of "the use of knowledge in society," the title of the most famous essay by Hayek, whom Heyne greatly admired. This has significant implications for the study of economic theory and policy. For example, to Heyne the corporate takeover market is a mechanism that, among other things, tells us which kinds of corporate structures succeed and which do not. Indeed, allowing corporate restructurings to take place is the only way to gain such information. By contrast, too many other economists (and especially non-economists), because they fail to understand this straightforward point, condemn the takeover market as wasteful and call for regulation.

The Economic Way of Thinking also explains why such "middlemen" as real estate agents, stockbrokers, and speculators, who are generally reviled by the politically correct, are in fact indispensable to the smooth operation of markets. The beneficial role of speculators, Heyne wrote, is to "even out the flow of commodities into consumption and diminish price fluctuations over time."

Paul Heyne devoted the last forty years of his life to teaching economics to students all over the world through his lectures and his outstanding textbook. His legacy to the economics profession is to have helped revive the study of markets as they should be studied: as institutions that facilitate, in Adam Smith's words, "man's propensity to truck, barter, and exchange," and not as an endless array of "optimization" problems and puzzles that are quickly forgotten.

EMBARKING ON A LIFELONG
PURSUIT OF KNOWLEDGE?

*Take Advantage of These New Resources
& a New Website*

The ISI Guides to the Major Disciplines are part of the Intercollegiate Studies Institute's (ISI) **Student Self-Reliance Project**, an integrated, sequential program of educational supplements designed to guide students in making key decisions that will enable them to acquire an appreciation of the accomplishments of Western civilization.

Developed with fifteen months of detailed advice from college professors and students, these resources provide advice in course selection and guidance in actual coursework. Project elements can be used independently by students to navigate the existing university curriculum in a way that deepens their understanding of our Western intellectual heritage, and its integrated components provide answers to the following fundamental questions at each stage of a student's education:

What are the strengths and weaknesses of the most selective schools?
Choosing the Right College directs prospective college students to the best and worst that top American colleges have to offer.

What is the essence of a liberal arts education?
A Student's Guide to Liberal Learning introduces students to the vital connection between liberal education and political liberty.

What core courses should every student take?
A Student's Guide to the Core Curriculum instructs students in building their own core curricula, utilizing electives available at virtually every university, and discusses how to identify and overcome contemporary political biases in those courses.

How can students learn from the best minds in their major field of study?
Student Guides to the Major Disciplines introduce students to overlooked and misrepresented classics, facilitating work within their majors. Guides currently available assess the fields of literature, philosophy, U.S. history, economics, and the study of history generally. Guides to political philosophy and sociology are currently in production.

Which great modern thinkers are neglected?
The Library of Modern Thinkers will introduce students to great minds who have contributed to the literature of the West and who are neglected or denigrated in today's classroom. Figures who make up this series include Robert Nisbet, Eric Voegelin, Wilhelm Röpke, Ludwig von Mises, Michael Oakeshott, Andrew Nelson Lytle, and many more.

In order to address the academic problems faced by every student in an ongoing manner, a new website, **www.collegeguide.org**, was recently launched. It offers easy access to unparalleled resources for making the most of one's college experience, and it features an interactive component that will allow students to pose questions about academic life on America's college campuses.

These features make ISI a one-stop organization for serious students of all ages. Visit **www.isi.org** or call **1-800-526-7022** and consider adding your name to the 50,000-plus ISI membership list of teachers, students, and professors.